WILD WHEELS

CHEVELLES

By Michael Portman

 Gareth Stevens
Publishing

Please visit our Web site, www.garethstevens.com. For a free color catalog of all our high-quality books, call toll free 1-800-542-2595 or fax 1-877-542-2596.

Library of Congress Cataloging-in-Publication Data

Portman, Michael, 1976-
 Chevelles / Michael Portman.
   p. cm. – (Wild wheels)
Includes index.
 ISBN 978-1-4339-4744-5 (pbk.)
 ISBN 978-1-4339-4745-2 (6-pack)
 ISBN 978-1-4339-4743-8 (library binding)
1. Chevelle automobile. 2. Chevelle automobile–History. I. Title.
TL215.C48P67 2011
629.222'2–dc22

                              2010038391

First Edition

Published in 2011 by
Gareth Stevens Publishing
111 East 14th Street, Suite 349
New York, NY 10003

Copyright © 2011 Gareth Stevens Publishing

Designer: Christopher Logan
Editor: Therese Shea

Photo credits: Cover and p. 1 (Chevelle and background), pp. 2-3 (background), 30-32 (background), back cover (engine), 2-32 (flame border), 4-5, 6-7, 12 (engine), 14-15, 24-25, 28-29 (sunset) Shutterstock.com; pp. 8-9, 26-27 © Kimball Stock Photo; pp. 10-11, 12-13, 16-17, 18-19, 20-21, 22-23, 28-29 (car) iStockphoto.com.

Printed in the United States of America

CPSIA compliance information: Batch #CW11GS: For further information contact Gareth Stevens, New York, New York at 1-800-542-2595.

CONTENTS

Strongmen 4

The Big Boys 6

Birth of the Super Sport 8

The Right Fit 10

Bulking Up 12

On Its Own 14

Ups and Downs 16

A New Look 18

Sales Giant 20

King of the Mountain 22

Back to Earth 26

Legacy 28

Glossary 30

For More Information 31

Index 32

Words in the glossary appear in **bold** type the first time they are used in the text.

Strongmen

In the 1960s and early 1970s, muscle cars ruled America's roads. Fast cars with powerful engines were nothing new. Some people— known as "hot rodders"—had been putting big engines into their cars for years. The muscle car was different. It came right from the factory with power. Without any changes, these cars could outperform many of the heavily reconstructed hot rods.

During the 1960s, the youth market was rapidly growing. Muscle cars' performances and prices made them hot products. Few muscle cars from any company were more successful than the Chevrolet Chevelle.

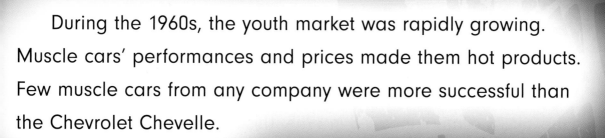

INSIDE THE MACHINE

The muscle cars of the 1960s sprang from two popular types of motorsports: drag racing and stock car racing. Drag races—speed races on a quarter-mile (400-m) track—were extremely popular in Southern California. Stock car racing, which used factory-built cars to race long distances, was popular in the southern United States.

Most muscle cars, such as the Chevelle pictured here, were two-door, midsize, and affordable.

5

The Big Boys

Chevrolet had been known for building high-performance engines since the introduction of their **V-8** in 1955. This fast, lightweight, and easily maintained engine was extremely popular with hot rodders and street racers. It became the most successful engine in the history of NASCAR (National Association for Stock Car Auto Racing).

Powerful engines, such as the one shown here, were essential in creating the legendary muscle car.

As popular as these engines were, it was the V-8 **big-block engine** that made Chevy muscle cars the stuff of legend. In 1961, the Chevrolet Impala Super Sport became the first car powered by Chevy's V-8 big-block engine, the 409. The 409 proved to be a powerful engine and was even the subject of the popular Beach Boys song, "409."

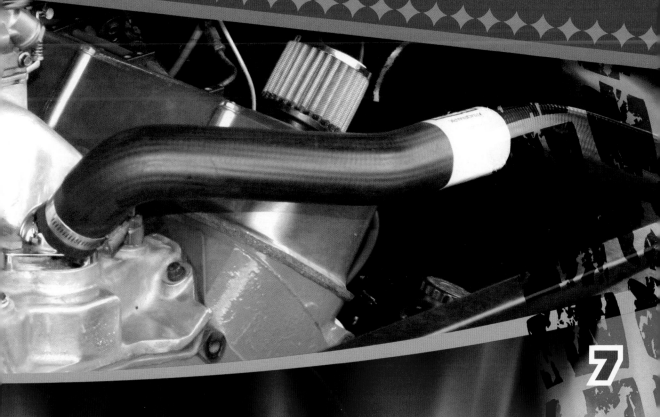

INSIDE THE MACHINE

Despite recording many songs about them, the Beach Boys didn't know much about cars, engines, or racing. According to founding member Brian Wilson, no one in the band actually attended the popular Southern California drag races. Even so, their song helped make Chevy's big-block engine popular.

Birth of the Super Sport

The Chevrolet Impala Super Sport was one of Chevy's earliest muscle cars. The Impala was a full-size car first introduced in 1958. When it was restyled in 1961, the Impala became the first Chevrolet to be offered with a Super Sport, or SS, package. The SS package included improvements to the car inside and outside. Customers could choose between a handful of engines, including the powerful 409. As America's love of the muscle car grew, the Super Sport became increasingly popular. By the mid-1960s, however, full-size cars were falling out of favor. Midsize muscle cars were taking over.

This 1961 Impala SS has special trim, or decorations and details on the inside and outside of the car, like the flags on the front.

INSIDE THE MACHINE

The 1964 Pontiac Tempest GTO set the standard for muscle cars of the mid-1960s. On the outside, the GTO appeared to be just an ordinary car, but under the hood was a powerful engine. Most muscle cars, including the Chevelle, followed the same pattern. Over the next few years, muscle cars would take on their own special look.

The Right Fit

Chevrolet was in need of a midsize car. The Impala was powerful but too big. The Chevy II and Corvair were too small. The 1964 Chevrolet Chevelle filled the gap nicely. The Chevelle came in a variety of styles: **coupes**, two-door and four-door **station wagons**, and four-door **sedans**.

Customers looking for a more "muscular" Chevelle were a little disappointed. The Super Sport package was offered as an addition to the Chevelle's top **trim level**, the Malibu. However, it lacked the high-**horsepower** engines that powered the Impala.

The 1965 Chevrolet Impala (shown here) was long, and it weighed over 4,200 pounds (1,907 kg). It didn't fit the midsize label.

INSIDE THE MACHINE

Chevrolet created the Chevelle to compete against midsize cars such as the Ford Fairlane offered in 1962. Most car companies saw that there was a high demand for midsize cars. They quickly created their own. Chevrolet was one of the last companies to issue a midsize car.

Bulking Up

While other General Motors (GM) manufacturers were putting big-block engines into their muscle cars, the Chevelle remained loyal to Chevy's original V-8 engines. There was one exception. Offered midway through the 1965 model year, the limited-edition Chevelle Malibu SS Z-16 sported Chevy's new 396 big-block engine.

396 big-block engine

Chevrolet built 294,160 Chevelles during its first year of production.

The 396 was a new engine that replaced the famous 409. It was **designed** for Chevrolet's top-of-the-line sports car, the Corvette. Although only 201 Chevelle Malibu SS **hardtops** and **convertibles** received the Z-16 package, it was a turning point for the Chevelle SS as a muscle car.

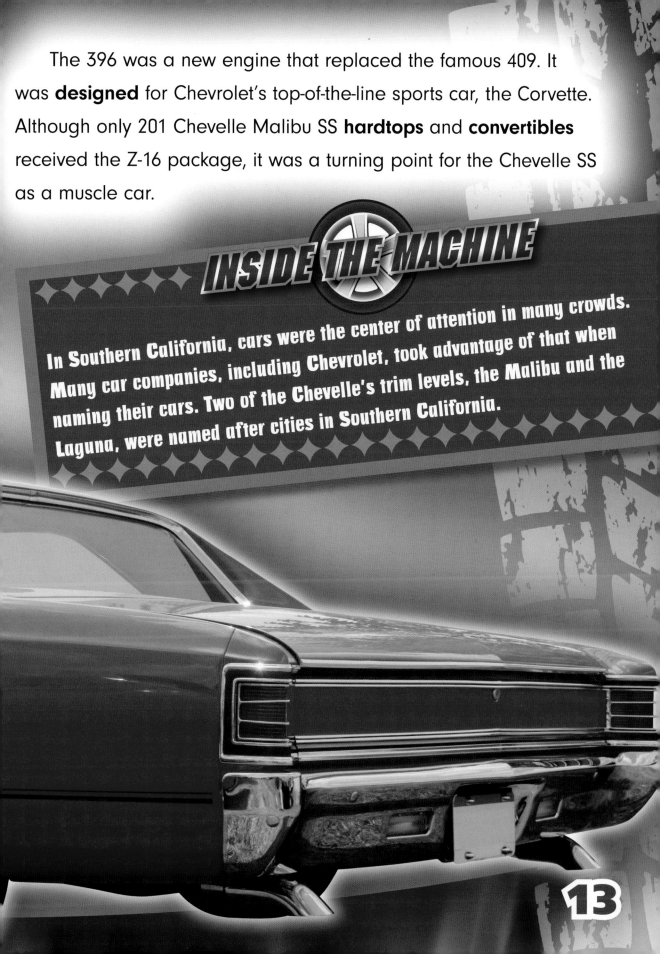

INSIDE THE MACHINE

In Southern California, cars were the center of attention in many crowds. Many car companies, including Chevrolet, took advantage of that when naming their cars. Two of the Chevelle's trim levels, the Malibu and the Laguna, were named after cities in Southern California.

On Its Own

In 1966, instead of the Super Sport package being added to the Malibu line, Chevy made the SS into its own line—the Chevelle SS 396. While customers could still choose an ordinary Chevelle from other trim levels, the Super Sport line featured true muscle cars.

In 1966, 412,155 Chevelles were produced. This was over 100,000 more than its first year!

When Chevy put the 396 engine into the 1965 Chevelle Malibu SS Z-16, it was a limited edition—only a few were produced. Now, every Chevelle SS came with a 396 engine. At first, the engines in the 1966 SS 396 weren't as powerful as the one used in the Z-16. Then, Chevrolet offered a 396 engine called the L78. The L78 pumped out a whopping 375 horsepower!

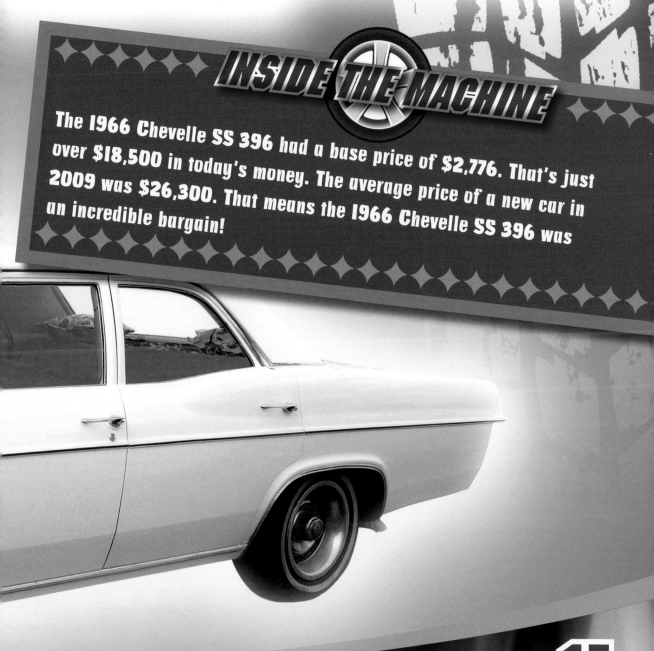

INSIDE THE MACHINE

The 1966 Chevelle SS 396 had a base price of $2,776. That's just over $18,500 in today's money. The average price of a new car in 2009 was $26,300. That means the 1966 Chevelle SS 396 was an incredible bargain!

Ups And Downs

In 1967, Chevrolet made several needed improvements to the Chevelle SS's road performance. Better tires gave the car a firmer grip on the pavement while turning. New front brakes reduced the Chevelle's stopping distance.

Instead of increasing the horsepower of the Chevelle SS 396's engines, Chevrolet decreased it. It was a strange direction to take for a muscle car in 1967, but the loss of power didn't really hurt sales figures.

Because of its head-turning style, the 1967 Chevelle SS sold well.

INSIDE THE MACHINE

From 1964 until 1977, the Chevrolet El Camino coupe was based on the Chevelle platform (or design, size, and power). The El Camino was called a utility vehicle. It was part car, part pickup truck. The front half of the El Camino was exactly like the Chevelle, while the back half was an open truck bed.

17

A New Look

In 1968, the Chevelle underwent a major design change. The **wheelbase** was shortened by 3 inches (7.6 cm). Past Chevelles had been full of sharp lines and angles. The new design was smooth and curvy.

Under the hood of the Chevelle SS, the three engine choices from 1967 had carried over. However, Chevy also offered a fourth choice, the 375-horsepower 396 L78 that was last seen in 1966. Because big-block engines were so heavy, cars that carried them were challenging to handle. The 1968 Chevelle SS was no exception.

INSIDE THE MACHINE

The full-size 1968 Chevy Impala had a wheelbase of 119 inches (302 cm), and the compact 1968 Chevy Corvair had a wheelbase of 108 inches (274 cm). The 1968 Chevelle SS 396 was right in the middle with a wheelbase of 112 inches (284 cm). That's why it was called a midsize car.

In 1968, the hood of the Chevelle was lengthened and the trunk shortened.

Sales Giant

In 1969, after 3 years as a separate trim level, Chevrolet turned the SS 396 into a special package. This time, though, it was offered on all Chevelle coupes and convertibles, not just the top-level Malibu. The Chevelle SS 396 was just as powerful as ever. Chevrolet decorated it inside and out with eye-catching "SS 396" **emblems**.

The 1969 Chevelle SS 396 sold a record 86,307 models, with more than 9,000 of them carrying the powerful 396 L78 engine. The muscle-car age was just about to reach its peak, and the Chevelle SS was ready to stand on the mountaintop.

INSIDE THE MACHINE

The Chevelle SS moved fast on the road and at the dealership. In 1968, Chevrolet made 57,600 Chevelle SS 396s. They produced 28,707 more 1969 models. Chevrolet built almost 296,000 SS 396s and SS 454s from 1968 to 1972. That's more than any other muscle car!

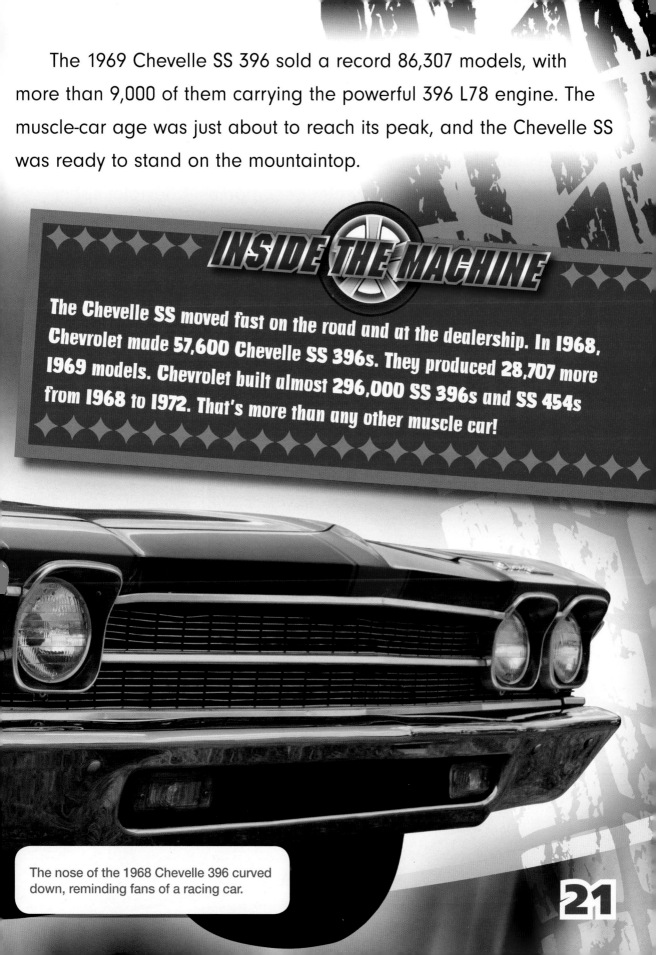

The nose of the 1968 Chevelle 396 curved down, reminding fans of a racing car.

King of the Mountain

When Chevrolet introduced the Chevelle SS in 1964, the Chevelle's small engines weren't ready to compete with the serious muscle machines produced by other companies. Chevrolet spent the next several years trying to fix that problem.

By 1970, muscle cars were everywhere. It wasn't easy to stand out from the crowd. Bright colors, racing stripes, and **spoilers** could make a car look fast, but they didn't make a difference where it really counted—under the hood. Chevrolet didn't need tricks for the Chevelle. It relied on horsepower. The power of the 1970 Chevelle SS 454 was enough to make everyone take notice.

INSIDE THE MACHINE

In 1970, Chevrolet restyled the Chevelle yet again. It had the same basic shape as the 1968 and 1969 models, but it had a simpler, cleaner look. Chevelle SS models could be ordered with two large racing stripes that ran from the hood to the trunk.

Though this 1970 Chevelle has a fancy paint job, its best feature was its powerful engine.

In 1970, Chevrolet's entry in the muscle-car wars was the Chevelle SS 454. The SS 454 package offered customers a choice of two engines—the LS5 and the LS6. The LS5 produced an exciting 360 horsepower. The LS6, on the other hand, produced an incredible 450 horsepower. The Chevelle SS 454 was not only the most powerful Chevelle ever, it was the most powerful muscle car!

454 engine

The Chevelle SS 454 was heavy, but even at 3,800 pounds (1,725 kg), it was still one of the fastest cars on the track. Other improvements gave the Chevelle SS 454 excellent handling for a car of its size.

INSIDE THE MACHINE

Customers could choose Chevy's cowl-induction system. This system placed a flap near the base of the windshield that opened when the driver pressed the gas pedal. The increased airflow allowed the engine to "breathe" and thus increased its performance.

The powerful 454 engine was named for its size—454 cubic inches.

Back to Earth

To test a car's performance, it's timed as it speeds from 0 to 60 miles (97 km) per hour. It's also timed to see how quickly it travels 1/4 mile (400 m). The 1970 Chevelle SS 454 LS6 took just 6.1 seconds to hit 60 miles per hour and just 13.7 seconds to finish 1/4 mile. Those were the fastest times it would ever record.

This Chevelle SS is from 1972, the last year Chevy used the 454 LS5 engine in this model. The LS6 was last used 2 years before.

The muscle-car age came to an end in the 1970s. Rising fuel costs caused a demand for more **fuel-efficient** cars. Chevrolet produced the Chevelle until 1977. In 1978, it was replaced by the Malibu, which was the name of Chevelle's most popular trim level.

INSIDE THE MACHINE

In 1972, Chevrolet issued a Chevelle SS called the Heavy Chevy. The Heavy Chevy looked like a powerful muscle car but lacked some of the features of a standard Chevelle SS. The powerful 454 LS6 engine was not a choice for the Heavy Chevy.

Legacy

There are countless opinions about which muscle car was the best. One thing is certain. In 1970, Chevrolet produced the most powerful muscle car to leave a factory, the Chevelle SS 454 LS6.

Today, muscle cars are rising again. People from across the world are committed to rebuilding and collecting classic muscle cars. The legendary 1970 SS 454 LS6 is one of the most sought-after muscle cars. In June 2010, a reconstructed SS 454 LS6 convertible sold for $253,000!

INSIDE THE MACHINE

In 2002, Chevrolet stopped production of the Camaro, their smaller muscle car. In 2009, the Camaro returned to production. Unfortunately, there are currently no plans to bring back the Chevelle, but muscle-car fans can always dream!

Though only offered by Chevy for a few years, the Chevelle will remain a classic example of an American muscle car.

Glossary

big-block engine: a large engine produced in the 1960s and 1970s

convertible: a car with a roof that can be lowered or removed

coupe: a two-door car with one section for the seat and another for storage space

design: to decide the pattern or shape of something

emblem: a sign that represents an object, idea, group, or quality

fuel-efficient: able to operate using little fuel, or without waste

hardtop: a two-door or four-door car without a center door post

horsepower: a measurement of an engine's power

sedan: a car with front and back seats, two or four doors, an enclosed body, and a permanent top

spoiler: a wing-shaped device attached to the back of a car to improve airflow and stability

station wagon: a car with an extended area behind the rear seats

trim level: the features and decorations included in a car's options package

V-8: an engine with eight cylinders, which are tube-shaped spaces with moving pistons

wheelbase: the distance between the centers of the front and rear wheels on a car

For More Information

Books

Mueller, Mike. *The Complete Book of Classic GM Muscle*. Minneapolis, MN: MBI Publishing, 2008.

Poolos, J. *Wild About Muscle Cars*. New York, NY: PowerKids Press, 2007.

Steffes, Jeffrey Dean. *Chevelle SS 1964–1972: A Muscle Car Source Book*. Watertown, MN: JC Publishing, 2007.

Web Sites

A Short Course on Automobile Engines
www.familycar.com/engine.htm
Find out how a car engine works and what different kinds exist.

Collisionkids.org
www.collisionkids.org
Learn about cars by playing games and completing related projects.

What's Inside: Muscle Cars
musclecars.howstuffworks.com/classic-muscle-cars/1970-chevrolet-chevelle-ss-454.htm
Read about the most powerful muscle car to ever hit the road.

Publisher's note to educators and parents: Our editors have carefully reviewed these Web sites to ensure that they are suitable for students. Many Web sites change frequently, however, and we cannot guarantee that a site's future contents will continue to meet our high standards of quality and educational value. Be advised that students should be closely supervised whenever they access the Internet.

Index

Beach Boys 7
big-block engines 6, 7, 12, 18

Chevelle Malibu SS Z-16 12, 13, 15
Chevelle platform 17
Chevelle SS 13, 14, 15, 16, 18, 21, 22, 23,
    26, 27
Chevelle SS 454 21, 22, 24, 25, 26, 28
Chevelle SS 396 14, 15, 16, 19, 20, 21
coupes 10, 20
cowl-induction system 25

drag racing 5, 7

El Camino 17

454 LS5 engine 24, 26
454 LS6 engine 24, 26, 27, 28
"409" 7
409 engine 7, 8, 13
full-size 8, 19

General Motors (GM) 12

Heavy Chevy 27
horsepower 10, 15, 16, 18, 22, 24
hot rodders 4, 6

Impala Super Sport (SS) 7, 8, 10
Laguna 13

Malibu 10, 13, 14, 20, 27
midsize 5, 8, 10, 11, 19
muscle cars 4, 5, 6, 7, 8, 9, 12, 13, 14, 16,
    21, 22, 23, 24, 27, 28, 29

NASCAR 6

performance testing 26

sedans 10
Southern California 5, 7, 13
spoilers 22
station wagons 10
stock car racing 5
Super Sport (SS) package 8, 10, 14

396 big-block engine 12, 13, 15
396 L78 engine 15, 18, 21
trim levels 10, 13, 14, 20, 27

V-8 engine 6, 7, 12

wheelbase 18, 19